MACHINE POLITICS
CHICAGO MODEL

From the "Chicago Tribune," February 7, 1931